pie
fresh from the oven

THE AUSTRALIAN
Women's Weekly

CONTENTS

AUSTRALIAN CUP AND SPOON MEASUREMENTS ARE METRIC.
A CONVERSION CHART APPEARS ON PAGE 77.

Pies are a family favourite – easy to make and delicious. Most of these recipes call for ready-made frozen pastry, bought from the supermarket. They are perfect for the busy family. For those with a bit more time there is a fantastic recipe for homemade shortcrust pastry, along with lots of helpful tips.

Pamela Clark

Food Director

PASTRY

Most types of pastry can be bought, ready-rolled, at the supermarket. Shortcrust pastry, however, is a lovely one to master at home. It's simple and satisfying to make. Follow a good basic recipe like the one below and be sure to read our helpful tips.

BASIC SHORTCRUST PASTRY

1½ cups (225g) plain (all-purpose) flour
125g (4 ounces) cold butter, chopped coarsely
1 egg yolk
2 tablespoons iced water, approximately

hand-made method

Sift flour into large bowl, rub in butter with fingertips. Add egg yolk and enough of the water to make ingredients barely cling together. Knead pastry lightly on floured surface until smooth; press into a disc shape. Enclose pastry in plastic wrap, refrigerate 30 minutes. Roll out.

processor method

Sift flour into processor bowl, add butter; pulse until mixture is crumbly. Add egg yolk and most of the water, pulse until ingredients barely cling together, add more water if necessary. Knead pastry lightly on floured surface until smooth; press into disc shape. Enclose pastry in plastic wrap, refrigerate 30 minutes. Roll out.

Sweet shortcrust pastry variation:

Sift 2 tablespoons icing (confectioners') sugar with the flour.

Note: **This recipe makes the equivalent of two sheets of store-bought shortcrust pastry.**

TIPS FOR MAKING PERFECT PASTRY

• Ideally, pastry should be made in a cool kitchen; all the ingredients and even the mixing bowl should be chilled. Cool fingertips with a light touch make good pastry, hot hands and heavy handling don't. Food processors make good pastry too, provided ingredients are "pulsed" together using short bursts of power. Over-handling or over-processing will result in tough pastry that can develop large cracks when rolled.

• Most recipes suggest only an approximate amount of liquid to add, due to the rate at which flour absorbs liquid. Old flour (more dehydrated) will absorb more liquid than new (less dehydrated) flour. Insufficient liquid will result in pastry that is crumbly and almost impossible to roll out. Too much liquid will make the pastry too soft and the pastry will shrink during baking.

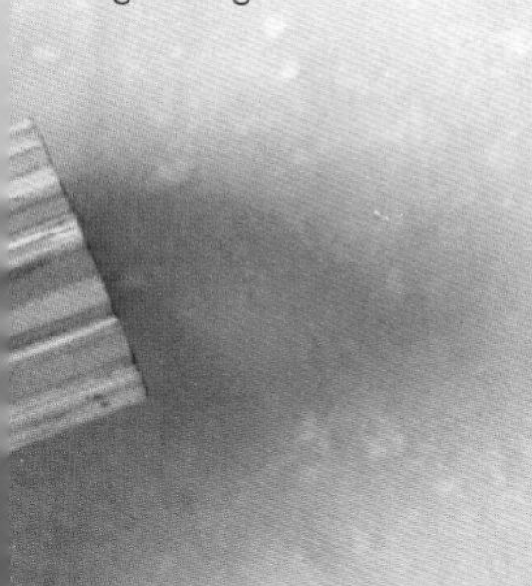

• Resting pastry in the refrigerator is vital for success. During this time, the protein (gluten) in the flour relaxes, resulting in a pastry with delicious texture. It also helps to minimise shrinkage during baking.

• It's important, when pastry is being rolled out, that an even pressure is used to keep it the same thickness all the way through. Roll in short light strokes from the centre out to the edge.

• When lining a dish or tin with pastry, gently push the pastry around the side of the dish, without stretching it; stretched pastry will shrink during baking.

• Some recipes require the pastry to be "docked" (pricking the pastry all over, about 2cm / ¾ inch apart, using a fork or a pastry docker) to prevent it from rising during baking.

• Sometimes it is necessary to bake the pastry blind (i.e. cook it without a filling). Line the uncooked pastry case with a piece of baking paper, fill with uncooked rice or ceramic or metal beads. This is to weight the pastry evenly to prevent rising during baking.

PRETTY PIES

Pinching pastry edges not only keeps pie fillings contained, it's decorative too. Edges can be crimped or pressed with the tines of a fork, pinched with fingertips to make indents and frills or cut neatly with a round (or fluted round) cutter for small pie tops.

Rather than throwing pastry trimmings away, re-roll them and use them for decorative pie tops. Cut rolled pastry into strips and lay across the tops of pies to create a lattice pattern or cut out shapes (perhaps shapes that indicate the filling) and attach them to the tops of pies with some beaten egg.

COMMON PASTRY TYPES

shortcrust

A crumbly, tender pastry made either sweet or savoury. Used mainly for pies, tarts and flans.

puff

A versatile pastry that once cooked, becomes light, crispy and layered. Often used for pies, sausage rolls, pasties and slices.

fillo

Paper thin, opaque sheets of pastry, brushed with melted butter or oil and layered. Once cooked, becomes crisp and flaky. Greek in origin, fillo is used to make quiche, strudel, some pies and Mediterranean and Middle Eastern specialties.

COUNTRY CHICKEN AND VEGETABLE PIE

prep + cook time 50 minutes (+ cooling) **serves** 4
nutritional count per serving 29.9g total fat (8g saturated fat); 2441kJ (584 cal); 33.2g carbohydrate; 38.2g protein; 4.7g fibre

2 tablespoons olive oil
500g (1 pound) chicken breast fillets, chopped coarsely
1 medium brown onion (150g), chopped coarsely
1 large carrot (180g), chopped coarsely
1 celery stalk (150g), trimmed, chopped coarsely
150g (5½ ounces) button mushrooms, sliced thickly
2 medium potatoes (400g), chopped coarsely
1 tablespoon plain (all-purpose) flour
½ cup (125ml) dry white wine
1 cup (250ml) chicken stock
⅓ cup (80ml) pouring cream
½ cup (60g) frozen peas
2 tablespoons coarsely chopped fresh flat-leaf parsley
1 sheet puff pastry
1 egg, beaten lightly

1 Preheat oven to 220°C/425°F. Oil 1.5-litre (6-cup) ovenproof dish.
2 Heat half the oil in large saucepan; cook chicken until browned lightly. Remove from pan.
3 Heat remaining oil in same pan; cook onion, carrot, celery and mushrooms, stirring, until vegetables soften. Add potato, cook for 1 minute. Add flour; cook, stirring, until mixture bubbles and thickens. Gradually stir in wine; boil, stirring, 1 minute. Return chicken to pan with stock; bring to the boil. Reduce heat; simmer, uncovered, about 8 minutes until potato is tender. Stir in cream, peas and parsley; season to taste. Cool.
4 Spoon mixture into dish. Top with pastry. Trim edge; brush pastry with egg. Bake pie about 20 minutes or until browned lightly.

SAVOURY PIES

CHICKEN, MUSHROOM AND TARRAGON PIES

prep + cook time **1 hour 10 minutes (+ refrigeration & cooling)** makes **4**
nutritional count per pie **52.6g total fat (28.4g saturated fat); 3532kJ (845 cal); 43.9g carbohydrate; 48.9g protein; 3.5g fibre**

40g (1½ ounces) butter
200g (6½ ounces) button mushrooms, sliced thinly
750g (1½ pounds) chicken thigh fillets, chopped coarsely
1 tablespoon plain (all-purpose) flour
¾ cup (180ml) chicken stock
1 tablespoon finely chopped fresh tarragon
1 egg, beaten lightly

tarragon pastry

1½ cups (225g) plain (all-purpose) flour
¼ cup (20g) finely grated parmesan cheese
2 tablespoons finely chopped fresh tarragon
125g (4 ounces) butter, chopped coarsely
1 egg
1 tablespoon iced water, approximately

1 Make tarragon pastry.
2 Meanwhile, melt butter in large frying pan; cook mushrooms, stirring, until browned. Add chicken; cook, stirring, until browned. Add flour; cook, stirring, 1 minute. Gradually stir in stock; stir over heat until mixture boils and thickens. Season to taste; cool. Stir in tarragon.
3 Preheat oven to 200°C/400°F. Oil four (1-cup/250ml) metal pie tins. Divide pastry in half. Roll one half between sheets of baking paper until large enough to line tins. Cut pastry into four squares, lift into tins, press into base and sides; trim edges.
4 Divide chicken mixture between pies. Roll remaining pastry between sheets of baking paper. Cut four 14cm (5½-inch) rounds from pastry; place over chicken mixture. Press edges to seal. Refrigerate 20 minutes.
5 Brush tops with egg; cut a slit in pies. Bake about 30 minutes or until browned lightly. Stand in pans 5 minutes.

tarragon pastry Process flour, cheese, tarragon and butter until crumbly. Add egg and enough of the water to make ingredients just come together. Knead dough on floured surface until smooth. Enclose in plastic wrap; refrigerate 30 minutes.

CHICKEN, FENNEL AND CELERY PIE

prep + cook time **1 hour 30 minutes (+ refrigeration & cooling)** serves **4**
nutritional count per serving **47.4g total fat (27g saturated fat); 3390kJ (811 cal); 49g carbohydrate; 45.1g protein; 5.8g fibre**

1 tablespoon olive oil
1 medium fennel bulb (300g), trimmed, sliced thinly
2 celery stalks (300g), trimmed, chopped coarsely
1 medium leek (350g), chopped coarsely
600g (1½ pounds) chicken breast fillets, chopped coarsely
1 clove garlic, crushed
2 tablespoons plain (all-purpose) flour
1 cup (250ml) chicken stock
½ cup (125ml) pouring cream
1 egg white

sour cream pastry

1½ cups (225g) plain (all-purpose) flour
80g (2½ ounces) cold butter, chopped coarsely
⅓ cup (80g) sour cream
1 egg yolk

1 Make sour cream pastry.

2 Meanwhile, heat oil in large saucepan, cook fennel, celery and leek, stirring, until softened. Add chicken and garlic; cook, stirring, until chicken is browned lightly. Add flour; cook, stirring, until mixture thickens and bubbles. Gradually add combined stock and cream; cook, stirring, until mixture boils and thickens. Reduce heat; simmer, uncovered, about 10 minutes or until thickened. Season to taste. Transfer to 1.5-litre (6-cup) ovenproof dish. Cool 20 minutes.

3 Preheat oven to 200°C/400°F.

4 Roll pastry between sheets of baking paper until large enough to cover dish. Cover dish with pastry, trim edges. Seal edges with fork; use pastry scraps to decorate pie. Brush pastry with egg white. Bake about 45 minutes or until browned.

sour cream pastry Process flour and butter until crumbly. Add sour cream and egg yolk; process until ingredients just come together. Knead pastry on floured surface until smooth. Enclose in plastic wrap; refrigerate 30 minutes.

tip **Sour cream pastry is lighter in texture but richer in flavour than basic shortcrust pastry. It is extremely easy to handle and may be used for both savoury and sweet pies.**

CHICKEN BASTILLA

prep + cook time **1 hour 45 minutes** serves **6**
nutritional count per serving **30.6g total fat (11.8g saturated fat); 1952kJ (467 cal); 14.6g carbohydrate; 33.1g protein; 2.4g fibre**

1 tablespoon olive oil
800g (1½ pounds) chicken thigh fillets, chopped coarsely
2 medium red onions (340g), sliced thinly
2 cloves garlic, crushed
1 fresh long green chilli, chopped finely
½ teaspoon saffron threads
2 teaspoons ground coriander
1 teaspoon ground ginger
1½ cups (375ml) chicken stock
½ cup (40g) flaked almonds, roasted
3 eggs, beaten lightly
½ cup each coarsely chopped fresh coriander (cilantro) and flat-leaf parsley
¼ cup coarsely chopped fresh mint
80g (2½ ounces) butter, melted
8 sheets fillo pastry
1 teaspoon icing (confectioners') sugar
½ teaspoon ground cinnamon

1 Heat half the oil in large frying pan; cook chicken, in batches, stirring occasionally, about 5 minutes or until browned. Remove from pan.
2 Heat remaining oil in pan; cook onion, stirring, until softened. Add garlic, chilli, and spices; cook, stirring, until fragrant. Return chicken to pan with stock; bring to the boil. Reduce heat; simmer, uncovered, about 20 minutes or until liquid has almost evaporated. Transfer to large bowl; cool 5 minutes. Stir in nuts, egg and herbs; season.
3 Preheat oven to 200°C/400°F. Brush deep 20cm (8-inch) round cake pan with a little butter. Line an oven tray with baking paper.
4 Layer four sheets of pastry, brushing each with butter. Line cake pan with pastry, allowing edges to overhang. Repeat with remaining pastry and butter. Position pastry crossways over pastry in pan. Spoon chicken mixture into pan. Fold overhanging pastry over filling to enclose. Brush with butter.
5 Bake about 30 minutes or until browned. Turn pie onto tray. Bake about 15 minutes or until browned. Serve dusted with sifted icing sugar and cinnamon.

THAI GREEN CHICKEN CURRY PIES

prep + cook time **1 hour 25 minutes (+ cooling)** makes **4**
nutritional count per pie **41.2g total fat (18.4g saturated fat); 2830kJ (677 cal); 43.7g carbohydrate; 32.2g protein; 3.1g fibre**

- 1 tablespoon vegetable oil
- 500g (1 pound) chicken thigh fillets, chopped coarsely
- 1 medium potato (200g), chopped coarsely
- 1 tablespoon thai green curry paste
- ⅔ cup (160ml) light coconut milk
- ⅔ cup (160ml) water
- 1 tablespoon lime juice
- 100g (3 ounces) green beans, trimmed, chopped coarsely
- 2 tablespoons finely chopped fresh coriander (cilantro)
- 2 sheets shortcrust pastry
- 1 egg, beaten lightly

1 Heat oil in large saucepan; cook chicken, stirring, until browned. Add potato and paste; cook, stirring, until fragrant. Add coconut milk, the water and juice; bring to the boil. Reduce heat; simmer, uncovered, about 10 minutes or until potato is tender and sauce is thick. Remove from heat, stir in beans and coriander; season to taste. Cool 30 minutes.
2 Preheat oven to 200°C/400°F. Oil four holes of six-hole (¾-cup/180ml) texas muffin pan.
3 Cut four 13cm (5¼-inch) rounds and four 9cm (3¾-inch) rounds from pastry. Line base and side of pan holes with larger rounds. Divide chicken mixture between pastry cases.
4 Brush one side of smaller rounds with egg. Place egg-side down over filling. Press edges to seal; brush tops with egg. Use pastry scraps to decorate pies. Bake pies about 45 minutes or until browned lightly.

GREEK PRAWN PIES

prep + cook time **45 minutes (+ cooling)** makes **6**
nutritional count per pie **14.4g total fat (7.3g saturated fat); 1254kJ (300 cal); 21.3g carbohydrate; 18.5g protein; 2.2g fibre**

- 750g (1½ pounds) uncooked medium king prawns (shrimp)
- 1 tablespoon olive oil
- 1 medium brown onion (150g), chopped finely
- 2 cloves garlic, crushed
- 3 teaspoons plain (all-purpose) flour
- ¼ cup (60ml) dry white wine
- 410g (13 ounces) canned diced tomatoes
- 2 tablespoons finely chopped fresh flat-leaf parsley
- 12 sheets fillo pastry
- 60g (2 ounces) butter, melted
- 50g (1½ ounces) fetta cheese, crumbled

1 Shell and devein prawns.
2 Heat oil in large frying pan; cook onion and garlic, stirring, until onion softens. Add flour; cook, stirring, 1 minute. Add wine and undrained tomatoes; bring to the boil, stirring. Reduce heat; simmer, uncovered, about 3 minutes or until sauce thickens slightly. Add prawns and parsley; cook 1 minute. Season to taste. Cool.
3 Preheat oven to 200°C/400°F. Oil six-hole (¾-cup/180ml) texas muffin pan.
4 Layer two sheets of pastry, brushing each with butter. Fold in thirds to enclose buttered side. Brush with butter, fold in half, forming a square; brush with butter. Gently press into pan hole. Repeat with remaining pastry and butter.
5 Bake pastry cases about 5 minutes or until browned lightly.
6 Divide prawn mixture between pastry cases; top with cheese. Bake about 10 minutes or until browned lightly. Stand 5 minutes before serving.

tip **Serve with lemon wedges.**

SMOKED COD AND CHEDDAR PIE

prep + cook time **40 minutes** serves **4**
nutritional count per serving **38.2g total fat (15.9g saturated fat); 3122kJ (747 cal); 28.3g carbohydrate; 69.2g protein; 1.3g fibre**

500g (1 pound) smoked cod
2⅓ cups (580ml) milk
1 dried bay leaf
30g (1 ounce) butter
1 medium brown onion (150g), chopped finely
200g (6½ ounces) speck, chopped finely
2 tablespoons plain (all-purpose) flour
⅓ cup (80ml) dry white wine
½ cup (60g) coarsely grated cheddar cheese
2 tablespoons finely chopped fresh chives
400g (12½ ounces) firm white fish fillets, chopped coarsely
1 sheet puff pastry
1 egg, beaten lightly

1 Preheat oven to 220°C/425°F. Oil 1.5-litre (6-cup) ovenproof dish.
2 Place cod in large saucepan with 1⅓ cups (330ml) of the milk and bay leaf. Bring to the boil; simmer, uncovered, 5 minutes. Drain; discard milk and bay leaf. Flake fish; discard skin and bones.
3 Heat butter in same pan; cook onion and speck, stirring, until onion softens. Add flour; cook, stirring, until mixture bubbles and thickens. Gradually add wine; simmer, uncovered, 1 minute. Gradually stir in remaining milk; simmer, uncovered, 1 minute. Remove from heat; stir in cheese, chives and all fish. Season to taste.
4 Spoon mixture into dish. Top with pastry, trim edge. Use pastry scraps to decorate pie. Brush pastry with egg. Bake about 20 minutes or until browned.

tip **We used ling in this recipe, but any firm white fish fillet is fine.**

FISH PIES WITH POTATO SCALES TOPPING

prep + cook time **1 hour 15 minutes (+ refrigeration & cooling)** makes **6**
nutritional count per pie **38g total fat (23.7g saturated fat); 2475kJ (592 cal); 37g carbohydrate; 24.9g protein; 2.7g fibre**

2 medium potatoes (400g)
40g (1½ ounces) butter
1 small leek (200g), sliced thinly
¼ cup (35g) plain (all-purpose) flour
1 cup (250ml) pouring cream
500g (1 pound) thick white boneless fish fillets, chopped coarsely
2 tablespoons finely chopped fresh flat-leaf parsley
20g (¾ ounce) butter, melted, extra

shortcrust pastry

1½ cups (225g) plain (all-purpose) flour
80g (2½ ounces) butter
1 egg
2 tablespoons iced water, approximately

1 Make shortcrust pastry.
2 Boil or steam whole unpeeled potatoes about 20 minutes or until tender. Drain; cool. Peel potatoes; slice thinly.
3 Meanwhile, melt butter in medium saucepan; cook leek, stirring, until soft. Add flour; cook, stirring, 1 minute. Gradually stir in cream; stir over heat until mixture boils and thickens. Season to taste, cool. Stir in fish and parsley.
4 Preheat oven to 200°C/400°F. Oil six 1-cup (250ml) ovenproof dishes.
5 Roll pastry between sheets of baking paper until large enough to line dishes. Lift pastry into dishes, ease into bases and sides; trim edges. Prick bases well; place dishes on oven tray. Refrigerate 30 minutes.
6 Bake pastry cases 15 minutes. Cool.
7 Spoon fish mixture into pastry cases. Top with slightly overlapping potato slices; brush with extra butter. Bake about 20 minutes or until browned. Stand 5 minutes before serving.

shortcrust pastry Process flour and butter until crumbly. Add egg and most of the water; process until ingredients just come together. Knead pastry on floured surface until smooth. Enclose with plastic wrap; refrigerate 30 minutes.

tips **Serve with lemon wedges. We used blue-eye in this recipe, but any firm white fish fillet is fine.**

SALMON COULIBIAC

prep + cook time **1 hour (+ refrigeration)** serves **6**
nutritional count per serving **41.8g total fat (24.5g saturated fat); 2567kJ (614 cal); 43.7g carbohydrate; 15.7g protein; 2.1g fibre**

1 cup (150g) cooked white rice
2 green onions (scallions), sliced thinly
2 hard-boiled eggs, mashed
1 tablespoon mayonnaise
1 tablespoon finely chopped fresh dill
210g (6½ ounces) canned red salmon, drained
1 egg, beaten lightly

shortcrust pastry

2 cups (300g) plain (all-purpose) flour
250g (8 ounces) cold butter, chopped coarsely
1 teaspoon finely grated lemon rind
¼ cup (60ml) iced water, approximately

1 Make shortcrust pastry.
2 Preheat oven to 220°C/425°F. Heat large oven tray.
3 Combine rice and onion in small bowl. Combine egg, mayonnaise and dill in small bowl; season. Remove skin and bones from salmon; mash.
4 Cut one third of pastry from block; refrigerate. Roll remaining pastry between sheets of baking paper until 20cm x 26cm (8 inches x 10½ inches).
5 Spoon rice mixture over pastry, leaving a 3cm (1¼-inch) border. Top with salmon then egg mixture.
6 Roll refrigerated pastry until 24cm x 29cm (9½ inches x 11½ inches). Mark a rectangle 2cm (¾ inch) in from edge of pastry. Put pastry over filling, pressing edges together. Mark lines across pastry. Brush with egg.
7 Bake on hot tray about 20 minutes or until browned. Stand 5 minutes.
shortcrust pastry Pulse flour, butter and rind five times in processor; turn onto flat surface. Knead in enough of the water until pastry just comes together. Enclose in plastic wrap; refrigerate 30 minutes.

CHUNKY BEEF AND MUSHROOM PIES

prep + cook time **2 hours (+ cooling & refrigeration)**
makes **6**
nutritional count per pie (with sauce) **53.8g total fat (17.1g saturated fat); 3992kJ (955 cal); 77.9g carbohydrate; 36.6g protein; 7.5g fibre**

600g (1¼ pounds) beef chuck steak, chopped coarsely
2 tablespoons plain (all-purpose) flour
2 tablespoons olive oil
1 small brown onion (80g), chopped finely
2 cloves garlic, crushed
125g (4 ounces) mushrooms, chopped coarsely
410g (13 ounces) canned crushed tomatoes
¾ cup (180ml) beef stock
2 tablespoons tomato paste
2 tablespoons worcestershire sauce
3 sheets shortcrust pastry
2 sheets puff pastry
1 egg, beaten lightly

tomato sauce

1 tablespoon olive oil
1 medium brown onion (150g), chopped coarsely
2 tablespoons light brown sugar
800g (1½ pounds) canned crushed tomatoes
1 teaspoon ground allspice
2 tablespoons tomato paste
¼ cup (60ml) white wine vinegar

1 Coat beef in flour; shake off excess. Heat half the oil in large saucepan; cook beef, in batches, until browned. Remove from pan.

2 Heat remaining oil in same pan; cook onion, garlic and mushrooms, stirring, until vegetables soften. Return beef to pan with undrained tomatoes, stock, paste and sauce; bring to the boil. Reduce heat; simmer, covered, 1 hour. Uncover; simmer about 15 minutes or until thickened slightly. Season to taste; cool.

3 Meanwhile, make tomato sauce.

4 Oil six ⅔-cup (160ml) pie tins; place on oven tray. Cut six 13cm (5¼-inch) rounds from shortcrust pastry. Ease pastry into tins, press into base and sides; trim edges. Refrigerate 30 minutes.

5 Preheat oven to 200°C/400°F.

6 Line pastry with baking paper; fill with dried beans or rice. Bake 10 minutes; remove paper and beans. Bake further 5 minutes; cool.

7 Cut six 11cm (4½-inch) rounds from puff pastry. Fill pastry cases with beef filling; brush edges with egg. Top with puff pastry rounds; press edges to seal. Brush tops with egg; cut steam holes in tops. Bake about 25 minutes or until browned lightly. Serve with tomato sauce.

tomato sauce Heat oil in medium saucepan; cook onion, stirring, until soft. Add sugar, undrained tomatoes and allspice; bring to the boil. Reduce heat; simmer, uncovered, stirring occasionally, about 30 minutes or until mixture thickens. Stir in paste and vinegar; cook, uncovered, 5 minutes. Blend or process sauce until smooth. Push through fine sieve into medium bowl; discard solids. Cool.

BEEF SHIRAZ PIES

prep + cook time **3 hours (+ cooling & refrigeration)**
makes **6**
nutritional count per pie **45.7g total fat (21.6g saturated fat); 3202kJ (766 cal); 46.5g carbohydrate; 37.1g protein; 4.4g fibre**

750g (1½ pounds) beef chuck steak, chopped coarsely
2 tablespoons plain (all-purpose) flour
¼ cup (60ml) olive oil
1 medium brown onion (150g), chopped finely
1 medium carrot (120g), chopped finely
2 celery stalks (300g), trimmed, chopped finely
2 cloves garlic, crushed
½ cup (125ml) dry red wine
½ cup (125ml) beef stock
410g (13 ounces) canned diced tomatoes
2 tablespoons fresh thyme leaves
1 egg, beaten lightly
sour cream pastry
2¼ cups (335g) plain (all-purpose) flour
125g (4 ounces) cold butter, chopped coarsely
½ cup (120g) sour cream

1 Preheat oven to 180°C/350°F. Oil six-hole (¾-cup/180ml) texas muffin pan.
2 Toss beef in flour, shake away excess. Heat half the oil in large frying pan; cook beef, in batches, until browned. Transfer beef to 3-litre (12-cup) ovenproof dish.
3 Heat remaining oil in same pan; cook onion, carrot, celery and garlic, stirring, until softened. Add wine; bring to the boil. Stir in stock, undrained tomatoes and thyme; bring to the boil. Pour over beef. Cook, covered, in oven, 2 hours. Season to taste; cool.
4 Meanwhile, make sour cream pastry.
5 Roll two-thirds of the pastry between sheets of baking paper until large enough to cut six 13cm (5-inch) rounds; press pastry into pan holes. Brush edges with egg. Divide beef mixture between pastry cases.
6 Cut six 9cm (3½-inch) rounds from remaining pastry; place pastry over filling. Press edges firmly to seal; brush tops with egg. Cut a small slit in top of each pie.
7 Bake pies about 30 minutes or until browned. Stand pies 5 minutes before serving.
sour cream pastry Process flour and butter until crumbly. Add sour cream; process until ingredients barely cling together. Knead dough on floured surface until smooth. Enclose in plastic wrap; refrigerate 30 minutes.

tip **Sour cream pastry is lighter in texture but richer in flavour than basic shortcrust pastry. It is easy to handle and may be used for both savoury and sweet pies.**

COTTAGE PIE

prep + cook time **1 hour 15 minutes (+ cooling & refrigeration)** serves **6**
nutritional count per serving **35.8g total fat (16.9g saturated fat); 2533kJ (606 cal); 43.8g carbohydrate; 26.2g protein; 3.4g fibre**

2 tablespoons olive oil
1 medium brown onion (150g), chopped finely
1 medium carrot (120g), chopped finely
500g (1 pound) minced (ground) beef
2 tablespoons plain (all-purpose) flour
¾ cup (180ml) beef stock
2 tablespoons tomato sauce (ketchup)
1 tablespoon worcestershire sauce
2 tablespoons finely chopped fresh flat-leaf parsley
2 sheets shortcrust pastry
600g (1¼ pounds) potatoes, chopped coarsely
40g (1½ ounces) butter
½ cup (125ml) hot milk
⅓ cup (40g) coarsely grated cheddar cheese

1 Heat oil in large frying pan; cook onion and carrot, stirring, until soft. Add beef; cook, stirring, until beef changes colour. Add flour; cook, stirring, 1 minute. Gradually stir in combined stock and sauces; stir over heat until mixture boils and thickens. Simmer, uncovered, 10 minutes; stir in parsley, season to taste, cool.
2 Preheat oven to 200°C/400°F. Oil 24cm (9½-inch) loose-based flan tin.
3 Cut one sheet of pastry in half. Join pieces to two sides of remaining pastry sheet. Lift pastry into tin, ease into base and side, trim edge; prick base all over with fork. Place on an oven tray. Refrigerate 20 minutes.
4 Bake pastry case 15 minutes. Cool. Spoon beef mixture into pastry case.
5 Boil or steam potato about 20 minutes or until soft; drain. Add butter and milk; mash until smooth, season to taste. Spoon mash over beef mixture; sprinkle with cheese.
6 Bake, uncovered, about 20 minutes or until browned. Stand pie 5 minutes before serving.

tip **You can use one quantity basic shortcrust pastry (page 4) instead of the store-bought pastry sheets.**

CURRIED BEEF AND PEA PIE

prep + cook time **45 minutes** serves **4**
nutritional count per serving **27.2g total fat (7.4g saturated fat); 2128kJ (509 cal); 26.1g carbohydrate; 38.5g protein; 3.6g fibre**

- 1 tablespoon olive oil
- 1 large brown onion (200g), chopped finely
- 4 cloves garlic, crushed
- 600g (1¼ pounds) minced (ground) beef
- 2 tablespoons curry powder
- 2 tablespoons plain (all-purpose) flour
- 2 tablespoons tomato paste
- 2 cups (500ml) beef stock
- ¾ cup (90g) frozen peas
- 1 sheet puff pastry
- 1 egg, beaten lightly

1 Preheat oven to 220°C/425°F. Oil 1.5-litre (6-cup) ovenproof dish.

2 Heat oil in large saucepan; cook onion and garlic, stirring, until onion softens. Add beef; cook, stirring, until browned.

3 Add curry powder; cook, stirring, until fragrant. Add flour; cook, stirring, until mixture bubbles and thickens. Add paste, gradually stir in stock; stir until mixture boils and thickens. Simmer, uncovered, 10 minutes. Stir in peas; season to taste.

4 Pour mixture into dish. Top with pastry; trim edge. Brush pastry with egg; sprinkle with a little extra curry powder.

5 Bake about 20 minutes or until pastry is puffed and browned lightly.

SAUSAGE, EGG AND BACON PIES

prep + cook time **50 minutes (+ cooling)** makes **6**
nutritional count per pie **45g total fat (21.1g saturated fat); 2847kJ (681 cal); 41.6g carbohydrate; 26.7g protein; 3.8g fibre**

3 rindless bacon slices (240g), halved
2 thick sausages (300g)
3 sheets shortcrust pastry
1 cup (260g) bottled tomato pasta sauce
6 eggs
2 green onions (scallions), sliced thinly

1 Preheat oven to 220°C/425°F. Oil six-hole (¾-cup/180ml) texas muffin pan.
2 Cook bacon in large frying pan until browned and crisp; drain on absorbent paper. Cook sausages in same pan until browned all over and cooked through; cool. Slice sausages thinly.
3 Cut two 13cm (5½-inch) rounds from each pastry sheet; press rounds into pan holes. Prick bases with fork. Line bases and sides of each pastry case with bacon. Top with sausage; pour over sauce. Bake 10 minutes.
4 Using a spoon, make an indent in sauce. Crack an egg carefully into each pie; bake about 15 minutes or until egg is set.
5 Serve sprinkled with onion.

SPICED CHORIZO AND BEAN PIES

prep + cook time 45 minutes makes 4
nutritional count per pie 35.2g total fat (14.1g saturated fat); 1868kJ (447 cal); 16.1g carbohydrate; 15.6g protein; 4.1g fibre

2 teaspoons olive oil
3 cured chorizo sausages (375g), halved, sliced thinly
1 medium red onion (170g), chopped finely
2 cloves garlic, crushed
¼ teaspoon dried chilli flakes
1 teaspoon each smoked paprika and ground cumin
410g (13 ounces) canned crushed tomatoes
⅓ cup (80ml) water
400g (12½ ounces) canned white beans, rinsed, drained
4 sheets fillo pastry
30g (1 ounce) butter, melted

1 Preheat oven to 220°C/425°F. Oil four 1¼-cup (310ml) ovenproof dishes.
2 Heat oil in large saucepan; cook chorizo until crisp. Remove from pan, reserving oil. Cook onion and garlic in same pan, stirring, until softened. Add spices; cook, stirring, until fragrant. Add undrained tomatoes, the water and beans. Simmer, uncovered, 5 minutes; season.
3 Spoon mixture into dishes.
4 Brush pastry sheets with butter. Scrunch and place over filling.
5 Bake pies about 15 minutes or until pastry is browned and crisp.

LAMB AND ROSEMARY PIES WITH SCONE TOPPING

prep + cook time **55 minutes** makes **4**
nutritional count per pie **36.8g total fat (19.2g saturated fat); 2822kJ (675 cal); 38.7g carbohydrate; 46.9g protein; 2g fibre**

2 teaspoons olive oil
5 thick lamb and rosemary sausages (750g)
1 medium brown onion (150g), chopped finely
1 tablespoon plain (all-purpose) flour
1¼ cups (310ml) chicken stock
1 tablespoon honey
2 tablespoons coarsely chopped fresh rosemary
1 tablespoon milk
4 sprigs fresh rosemary

scone topping
1 cup (150g) self-raising flour
60g (2 ounces) butter, chopped coarsely
¼ cup (20g) finely grated parmesan cheese
½ cup (125ml) milk, approximately

1 Preheat oven to 200°C/400°F. Oil four 1¼-cup (310ml) ovenproof dishes.

2 Heat oil in large frying pan; cook sausages until browned and cooked through. Remove from pan; slice thinly. Cook onion in same pan, stirring, until tender. Add flour; cook, stirring, until mixture bubbles and thickens. Stir in stock, honey and chopped rosemary; stir over heat until mixture boils and thickens. Simmer, uncovered, 3 minutes. Return sausage to pan; season to taste.

3 Meanwhile, make scone topping.

4 Spoon hot filling into dishes. Top with scone topping. Brush with milk; press a rosemary sprig into top of each pie. Bake about 25 minutes or until browned.

scone topping Place flour in medium bowl; rub in butter, stir in cheese. Stir in enough milk to make a soft sticky dough. Divide dough into four; knead into rounds to fit dishes.

LAMB SHANK PIES WITH CRUSHED PEAS AND FETTA

prep + cook time **3 hours 10 minutes (+ cooling & refrigeration)** makes **6**
nutritional count per pie [with crushed peas] **36g total fat (15.5g saturated fat); 2876kJ (688 cal); 45.3g carbohydrate; 42.1g protein; 7.6g fibre**

6 french-trimmed lamb shanks (1.5kg)
¼ cup (35g) plain (all-purpose) flour
1 tablespoon olive oil
2 medium brown onions (300g), chopped coarsely
2 medium carrots (240g), chopped coarsely
3 cloves garlic, crushed
½ teaspoon dried oregano
3 cups (750ml) salt-reduced chicken stock
1 cup (260g) bottled tomato pasta sauce
2 medium potatoes (400g), chopped coarsely
2 tablespoons lemon juice
2 tablespoons chopped fresh dill
2 sheets butter puff pastry
1 egg, beaten lightly
crushed peas and fetta
2½ cups (300g) frozen baby peas
1 tablespoon torn fresh mint leaves
1 tablespoon olive oil
⅓ cup (65g) crumbled fetta cheese

1 Preheat oven to 180°C/350°F.
2 Toss shanks in flour; shake away excess. Heat oil in medium flameproof dish; cook shanks until browned. Remove from dish.
3 Add onion and carrot to same dish; cook, stirring, until soft. Add garlic and oregano; cook, stirring, until fragrant. Add stock and sauce; bring to the boil. Return shanks to dish; cover tightly. Transfer to oven; cook for 1½ hours.
4 Add potato to dish, cover; cook, in oven, 30 minutes or until lamb and potato are tender. Stir in juice and dill; season. Cool 10 minutes.
5 Remove half the meat from the shanks; cut meat into smaller pieces. Refrigerate lamb mixture and shanks 3 hours or until cold. Remove fat from surface of dish.
6 Preheat oven to 220°C/425°F.
7 Divide lamb mixture and shanks among six 2-cup (500ml) deep ovenproof dishes, standing shanks upright in dishes. Cut out pastry slightly larger than the tops of the dishes. Cut a small cross in the centre of each pastry.
8 Place pastry over pies, inserting shank bone through cross in pastry. Brush pastry with egg. Place dishes on oven tray. Bake 20 minutes or until browned.
9 Meanwhile, make crushed peas and fetta, serve with pies.

crushed peas and fetta Boil, steam or microwave peas until tender; drain. Crush peas lightly with fork. Stir in mint and oil; season to taste. Gently stir in cheese.

tip **Serve with lemon wedges.**

ROGAN JOSH LAMB PIE WITH CORIANDER CHUTNEY

prep + cook time **3 hours (+ cooling)** serves **6**
nutritional count per serving **30.9g total fat (8g saturated fat); 2337kJ (559 cal); 26.8g carbohydrate; 40.9g protein; 4.7g fibre**

1kg (2 pounds) diced lamb shoulder
⅓ cup (50g) plain (all-purpose) flour
2 tablespoons vegetable oil
2 medium brown onions (300g), sliced thinly
½ cup (135g) rogan josh curry paste
410g (13 ounces) canned diced tomatoes
2 cups (500ml) salt-reduced beef stock
1 sheet puff pastry
2 teaspoons milk
¼ teaspoon cumin seeds

coriander chutney

1 tablespoon lemon juice
1 teaspoon sugar
pinch ground cumin
1 fresh long green chilli, chopped coarsely
1 cup firmly packed fresh coriander (cilantro) leaves
1 cup firmly packed fresh mint leaves
½ cup (140g) thick yogurt

1 Toss lamb in flour; shake away excess. Heat oil in large saucepan; cook lamb, in batches, until well browned. Remove from pan.
2 Add onion to same pan; cook, stirring, until softened. Add paste to pan; cook, stirring, until fragrant. Return lamb to pan with undrained tomatoes and stock; bring to the boil. Reduce heat; simmer, covered, 1½ hours. Simmer, uncovered, about 30 minutes or until tender. Season to taste; cool.
3 Preheat oven to 220°C/425°F.
4 Spoon curry into 24cm (9½-inch) pie dish (1.5-litre/6-cup). Score pastry in criss-cross pattern. Place pastry over filling; trim edge. Brush pastry with milk, sprinkle with seeds. Place on oven tray; bake, uncovered, about 30 minutes or until browned.
5 Meanwhile, make coriander chutney.
6 Serve pie with chutney.

coriander chutney Blend all ingredients until smooth; season to taste.

tip **Do ask the butcher for lamb shoulder, as what is sold as diced lamb is sometimes from the leg and will not be as tender.**

OLD-FASHIONED LAMB AND CELERIAC PIE

prep + cook time 3 hours (+ cooling & refrigeration)
serves 6
nutritional count per serving 37.7g total fat (18.4g saturated fat); 3060kJ (732 cal); 43g carbohydrate; 51.9g protein; 6.5g fibre

1.25kg (2½ pounds) diced lamb shoulder
½ cup (75g) plain (all-purpose) flour
2 tablespoons olive oil
1 large brown onion (200g), chopped coarsely
1 large carrot (180g), chopped coarsely
750g (1½ pounds) celeriac (celery root), trimmed, chopped coarsely
1½ cups (375ml) salt-reduced beef stock
2 teaspoons chopped fresh thyme
2 tablespoons chopped fresh flat-leaf parsley
1 egg, beaten lightly

shortcrust pastry
1½ cups (225g) plain (all-purpose) flour
125g (4 ounces) butter, chopped coarsely
1 egg yolk
2 tablespoons iced water, approximately

1 Toss lamb in flour; shake away excess. Heat oil in large saucepan; cook lamb, in batches, until browned. Remove from pan.
2 Add onion, carrot and celeriac to pan; cook, stirring, 5 minutes. Return lamb to pan with stock and herbs; simmer, covered, about 2 hours or until lamb is tender. Season to taste; cool.
3 Meanwhile, make shortcrust pastry.
4 Preheat oven to 180°C/350°F.
5 Spoon lamb mixture into 2-litre (8-cup) ovenproof dish; place on oven tray.
6 Roll pastry between sheets of baking paper until large enough to cover top of dish. Brush edge of dish with egg. Place pastry over filling, trim edge; pinch edge in decorative pattern. Brush pastry with egg. Bake about 35 minutes or until browned.

shortcrust pastry Process flour and butter until crumbly. Add egg yolk and most of the water; process until ingredients just come together. Knead pastry on floured surface until smooth, enclose with plastic wrap; refrigerate 1 hour.

tip Do ask the butcher for lamb shoulder, as what is sold as diced lamb is sometimes from the leg and will not be as tender.

MOROCCAN-STYLE LAMB PIES WITH HARISSA YOGURT

prep + cook time **3 hours 15 minutes** serves **8**
nutritional count per serving **22.2g total fat (10g saturated fat); 1981kJ (474 cal); 30.1g carbohydrate; 36.9g protein; 3.2g fibre**

1.25kg (2½ pounds) diced lamb shoulder
½ cup (75g) plain (all-purpose) flour
2 tablespoons olive oil
2 medium brown onions (300g), chopped finely
2 medium carrots (240g), chopped finely
2 cloves garlic, crushed
1 teaspoon each ground coriander, cumin, ginger and turmeric
1 cinnamon stick
1½ cups (375ml) beef stock
6 fresh dates (150g), seeded, chopped coarsely
1 tablespoon honey
2 tablespoons finely chopped fresh coriander (cilantro)
8 sheets fillo pastry
50g (1½ ounces) butter, melted
2 teaspoons sesame seeds
harissa yogurt
¾ cup (200g) thick yogurt
2 tablespoons harissa

1 Toss lamb in flour; shake away excess. Heat oil in large saucepan; cook lamb, in batches, until browned. Remove from pan.
2 Add onion and carrot to pan; cook, stirring, until soft. Add garlic and spices; cook, stirring, until fragrant. Return lamb to pan with stock; simmer, covered, 1½ hours.
3 Preheat oven to 220°C/425°F.
4 Simmer lamb, uncovered, about 30 minutes or until lamb is tender and sauce is thickened. Stir in dates, honey and coriander; season to taste.
5 Spoon mixture into eight 1-cup (250ml) ovenproof dishes. Brush each pastry sheet with butter, scrunch and place over filling. Sprinkle with seeds. Bake, uncovered, about 15 minutes or until browned.
6 Meanwhile, make harissa yogurt.
7 Serve pies with harissa yogurt.
harissa yogurt Combine yogurt and half the harissa in small bowl. Serve topped with remaining harissa.

tips **Do ask the butcher for lamb shoulder, as what is sold as diced lamb is sometimes from the leg and will not be as tender. Harissa is a Tunisian hot chilli paste, available in delicatessens and gourmet food stores. As every brand is different, add it gradually, a teaspoon at a time, until the desired heat is reached. We used a mild harissa.**

ROASTED GARLICKY PUMPKIN AND SAGE PIES

prep + cook time **1 hour 30 minutes (+ refrigeration & cooling)** makes **6**
nutritional count per pie **40g total fat (21.3g saturated fat); 2353kJ (563 cal); 36.2g carbohydrate; 14g protein; 3.5g fibre**

900g (1¾ pounds) butternut pumpkin, chopped coarsely
4 cloves garlic, unpeeled
1 tablespoon olive oil
3 eggs, beaten lightly
½ cup (125ml) pouring cream
¼ cup coarsely chopped fresh sage
75g (2½ ounces) fetta cheese
1½ tablespoons pine nuts

spicy pastry

1½ cups (225g) plain (all-purpose) flour
1 teaspoon ground coriander
1 teaspoon cumin seeds
125g (4 ounces) cold butter, chopped coarsely
1 egg yolk
2 tablespoons iced water, approximately

1 Preheat oven to 220°C/425°F.
2 Place pumpkin and garlic on baking-paper-lined oven tray, drizzle with oil. Bake about 20 minutes or until tender. Transfer to large bowl; cool 5 minutes. Squeeze garlic from skins. Mash pumpkin and garlic coarsely with a fork. Stir in egg, cream and sage; season.
3 Meanwhile, make spicy pastry.
4 Grease six 9cm x 12cm (3½-inch x 5-inch) oval pie tins. Divide pastry into six even pieces. Roll each piece between sheets of baking paper until large enough to line tins. Lift pastry into tins; press into side, trim edge. Refrigerate 20 minutes.
5 Reduce oven to 200°C/400°F. Place tins on oven tray; cover pastry with baking paper, fill with dried beans or rice. Bake 10 minutes. Remove paper and beans; bake about 5 minutes or until browned lightly. Cool.
6 Fill pastry cases with pumpkin mixture. Sprinkle with crumbled cheese and nuts. Bake about 35 minutes or until set and browned.
spicy pastry Process flour, spices and butter until crumbly. Add egg yolk and most of the water; process until ingredients just come together. Knead dough on floured surface until smooth, enclose pastry in plastic wrap; refrigerate 30 minutes.

SPICED GREEN PEA AND POTATO PASTIES

prep + cook time **1 hour (+ cooling)** makes **10**
nutritional count per pastie **25.7g total fat (12.6g saturated fat); 1868kJ (447 cal); 45g carbohydrate; 8g protein; 3.1g fibre**

1 tablespoon olive oil
2 medium brown onions (300g), sliced thinly
1 tablespoon caster (superfine) sugar
1 tablespoon moroccan seasoning
2 cloves garlic, crushed
1 teaspoon fresh thyme leaves
1 medium potato (200g), chopped coarsely
350g (11 ounces) butternut pumpkin, chopped coarsely
⅔ cup (80g) frozen peas
5 sheets shortcrust pastry
1 egg, beaten lightly
2 teaspoons sesame seeds

1 Heat oil in large frying pan; cook onion and sugar, stirring, about 15 minutes or until caramelised. Stir in seasoning, garlic and thyme. Cook, stirring, until fragrant; transfer to large bowl.
2 Meanwhile, boil, steam or microwave potato and pumpkin, separately, until tender; drain. Add potato, pumpkin and peas to bowl. Stir gently to combine; season to taste, cool.
3 Preheat oven to 200°C/400°F. Line oven trays with baking paper.
4 Cut 10 x 13cm (5¼-inch) rounds from pastry. Spoon ⅓ cup potato mixture onto each round; brush edges with egg. Bring pastry edges together to form a semi-circle. Pinch edges together to seal.
5 Place pasties on trays. Brush with egg; sprinkle with seeds. Bake about 30 minutes or until browned lightly.

MINI VEGETABLE CURRY PIES

prep + cook time **1 hour 10 minutes (+ cooling)** makes **12**
nutritional count per pie **22.3g total fat (7.1g saturated fat); 1555kJ (372 cal); 34.6g carbohydrate; 7g protein; 3.2g fibre**

- 1 tablespoon vegetable oil
- 2 green onions (scallions), sliced thinly
- 1 medium red capsicum (bell pepper) (200g), chopped finely
- 1 medium potato (200g), chopped finely
- 1 medium zucchini (120g), chopped finely
- 1 medium carrot (120g), chopped finely
- ⅓ cup (100g) mild curry paste
- 2 cups (500ml) vegetable stock
- 125g (4 ounces) canned corn kernels, drained
- ½ cup (80g) frozen peas
- 3 sheets shortcrust pastry
- 2 sheets puff pastry
- 1 egg, beaten lightly
- 1 teaspoon cracked black pepper

1 Heat oil in large frying pan; cook onion, capsicum, potato, zucchini and carrot, stirring, until softened. Stir in paste, cook until fragrant. Add stock; bring to the boil. Reduce heat to medium; simmer, uncovered, until potato is tender and stock evaporated. Stir in corn and peas, remove from heat; season to taste. Cool.
2 Preheat oven to 200°C/400°F. Oil a 12-hole (⅓-cup/80ml) muffin pan. Cut 12 x 9cm (3½-inch) rounds from shortcrust pastry. Line pan holes with pastry. Fill with vegetable mixture. Cut 12 x 7.5cm (3-inch) rounds from puff pastry. Brush one side of rounds with egg. Place rounds, egg side down over filling; press edges to seal. Brush tops with egg. Sprinkle with pepper.
3 Bake pies about 30 minutes or until browned. Stand 5 minutes before serving.

APPLE AND BERRY FILLO PIE

prep + cook time 45 minutes **serves** 6
nutritional count per serving 6.4g total fat (2.9g saturated fat); 681kJ (163 cal); 31.7g carbohydrate; 2.7g protein; 5.6g fibre

6 medium apples (900g), peeled, cored, sliced thinly
¼ cup (55g) caster (superfine) sugar
2 teaspoons cornflour (cornstarch)
2 teaspoons water
2 teaspoons vanilla extract
½ teaspoon ground cinnamon
300g (9½ ounces) frozen mixed berries
4 sheets fillo pastry
30g (1 ounce) butter, melted
¼ teaspoon ground cinnamon, extra
2 tablespoons flaked almonds

1 Preheat oven to 220°C/ 425°F. Grease 1-litre (4-cup) pie dish.
2 Combine apple and sugar in large saucepan. Bring to the boil; simmer, covered, about 8 minutes or until tender.
3 Blend cornflour with the water in small jug, stir into apple mixture with extract and cinnamon; stir gently over heat until mixture boils and thickens slightly. Stir in berries, spoon into dish.
4 Brush each sheet of pastry with butter. Scrunch and place over filling. Sprinkle with extra cinnamon and nuts.
5 Bake pie about 20 minutes until browned.

SWEET PIES

CITRUS-TRIO MERINGUE PIE

prep + cook time **40 minutes (+ refrigeration & cooling)**
serves **8**
nutritional count per serving **23.2g total fat (13.9g saturated fat); 1914kJ (458 cal); 59.5g carbohydrate; 4.3g protein; 0.6g fibre**

185g (6 ounces) plain sweet biscuits
90g (3 ounces) unsalted butter, melted
½ cup (75g) cornflour (cornstarch)
1¼ cups (275g) caster (superfine) sugar
¼ cup (60ml) each orange, lemon and lime juice
1 cup (250ml) water
80g (2½ ounces) unsalted butter, extra
3 eggs, separated
2 teaspoons each finely grated orange, lemon and lime rind

1 Grease 24cm (9½-inch) round, 2cm (¾-inch) deep loose-based flan tin.
2 Blend or process biscuits until fine. Transfer to medium bowl; stir in melted butter.
3 Press biscuit mixture evenly over base and side of tin, place on oven tray; refrigerate 30 minutes.
4 Combine cornflour and ½ cup (110g) of the sugar in medium saucepan; gradually stir in juices and the water until smooth. Stir over high heat until mixture boils and thickens. Reduce heat; simmer, stirring, 1 minute. Remove from heat; stir in extra butter, egg yolks and rind until butter melts. Cool 10 minutes.
5 Spread filling over biscuit base, cover; refrigerate 2 hours.
6 Preheat oven to 240°C/475°F.
7 Beat egg whites in small bowl with electric mixer until soft peaks form; gradually add remaining sugar, 1 tablespoon at a time, beating until sugar dissolves between additions.
8 Roughen surface of filling with a fork before piping with meringue. Spoon mixture into piping bag fitted with 1.5cm (½-inch) plain tube. Pipe meringue over filling. Bake about 5 minutes or until meringue is browned lightly.

tips **Finely grate the rind from citrus before juicing. The base and filling can be made and assembled up to a day in advance. Meringue topping is best made just before serving. Roughing the surface of the filling will help the meringue to cling to the filling.**

BLACK-AND-BLUE BERRY PIE

prep + cook time **1 hour 15 minutes (+ refrigeration & cooling)** serves **8**
nutritional count per serving **14g total fat (8.7g saturated fat); 1471kJ (352 cal); 49.9g carbohydrate; 4.9g protein; 4.8g fibre**

400g (12½ ounces) frozen blackberries
⅓ cup (75g) caster (superfine) sugar
2 tablespoons cornflour (cornstarch)
2 tablespoons water
250g (8 ounces) fresh blueberries
2 teaspoons finely grated lemon rind
½ teaspoon mixed spice
1 egg white
2 teaspoons demerara sugar

custard pastry

1½ cups (225g) plain (all-purpose) flour
¼ cup (35g) cornflour (cornstarch)
¼ cup (30g) custard powder
2 tablespoons icing (confectioners') sugar
125g (4 ounces) cold butter, chopped coarsely
1 egg yolk
1 tablespoon iced water, approximately

1 Make custard pastry.
2 Meanwhile, combine 1 cup of the blackberries and sugar in medium saucepan. Bring to the boil. Blend cornflour with the water in small jug. Stir into berry mixture, stir over heat until mixture boils and thickens. Cool. Stir in remaining blackberries, blueberries, rind and spice.
3 Roll two-thirds of the pastry between sheets of baking paper until large enough to line 24cm (9½-inch) round loose-based flan tin. Ease pastry into tin; trim edge. Reserve and refrigerate excess pastry. Refrigerate pastry case 30 minutes.
4 Preheat oven to 200°C/400°F.
5 Spoon filling into pastry case. Brush edge with egg white. Roll reserved pastry between sheets of baking paper until large enough to cover pie. Cut into 10 x 1.5cm (½-inch) wide strips. Place strips over pie, weaving in and out to make lattice pattern. Trim edges, pressing to seal; sprinkle with demerara sugar.
6 Bake about 50 minutes or until browned. Stand 10 minutes before serving.

custard pastry Process flours, custard powder, icing sugar and butter until crumbly. Add egg yolk and enough of the water until ingredients just come together. Knead pastry on floured surface until smooth, enclose in plastic wrap; refrigerate 30 minutes.

WHISKY-LACED FRUIT MINCE PIES

prep + cook time **1 hour (+ standing & refrigeration)**
makes **15**
nutritional count per pie **10g total fat (6.2g saturated fat); 836kJ (200 cal); 24.9g carbohydrate; 2.8g protein; 1.1g fibre**

⅓ cup (50g) raisins, chopped finely
¼ cup (40g) sultanas, chopped finely
¼ cup (40g) dried currants
1 small apple (130g), grated coarsely
⅓ cup (80ml) whisky
⅓ cup (75g) demerara sugar
1 teaspoon finely grated lemon rind
1 teaspoon ground cinnamon
40g (1½ ounces) frozen butter, grated coarsely
1 egg, beaten lightly
2 tablespoons demerara sugar, extra

cinnamon pastry

1½ cups (225g) plain (all-purpose) flour
½ teaspoon ground cinnamon
125g (4 ounces) butter, chopped coarsely
1 egg

1 To make fruit mince, combine dried fruit, apple, whisky, sugar, rind and cinnamon in medium bowl. Cover; stand 48 hours. Stir in butter.

2 Make cinnamon pastry.

3 Preheat oven to 180°C/350°F. Grease 15 holes of two 12-hole (2-tablespoon/40ml) deep flat-based patty pans.

4 Roll pastry between sheets of baking paper until large enough to line pans. Cut 15 x 7cm (2½-inch) rounds from pastry. Line pan holes with pastry, barely fill with fruit mince.

5 Cut 15 x 6cm (2¼-inch) rounds from pastry. Cut small rounds from centres of each round. Place over filling, press edges together. Brush pies with egg; sprinkle with extra sugar.

6 Bake pies about 30 minutes. Stand 5 minutes before transferring to a wire rack to cool.

cinnamon pastry Process flour, cinnamon and butter until crumbly. Add egg; process until ingredients just come together. Knead dough on floured surface until smooth, enclose with plastic wrap; refrigerate 30 minutes.

PEAR AND CINNAMON SUGAR LATTICE PIES

prep + cook time **1 hour 15 minutes (+ refrigeration & cooling)** makes **4**
nutritional count per pie **27.9g total fat (17.5g saturated fat); 2400kJ (574cal); 86.1g carbohydrate; 8.5g protein; 5.6g fibre**

3 large pears (990g), peeled, cored, sliced thinly
¼ cup (55g) caster (superfine) sugar
2 teaspoons cornflour (cornstarch)
1 teaspoon vanilla extract
1 egg white
½ teaspoon ground cinnamon

pastry

1½ cups (225g) plain (all-purpose) flour
2 tablespoons icing (confectioners') sugar
125g (4 ounces) cold butter, chopped coarsely
1 egg yolk
2 tablespoons iced water, approximately

1 Make pastry.

2 Grease four 10cm (4-inch) round loose-based flan tins. Divide pastry into five portions. Roll each of four portions between baking paper until large enough to line tins. Lift pastry into tins, press into sides; trim edges. Reserve pastry scraps with the fifth portion. Refrigerate 30 minutes.

3 Preheat oven to 180°C/350°F.

4 Meanwhile, combine pear and one-third of the sugar in medium saucepan. Cook, covered, until pear is tender. Drain, reserve 1 tablespoon liquid. Blend or process mixture until almost smooth. Return to pan with half the remaining sugar. Blend cornflour with reserved liquid; stir into pear mixture; stir over heat until mixture boils and thickens. Stir in extract; cool.

5 Spoon pear filling into pastry cases. Brush edges with egg white. Roll all reserved pastry between sheets of baking paper. Cut into 12 x 1cm (½-inch) wide strips. Weave strips over pies. Trim edges, pressing to seal; sprinkle with combined remaining sugar and cinnamon. Bake about 50 minutes.

pastry Process flour, icing sugar and butter until crumbly. Add egg yolk and enough of the water to make ingredients just come together. Knead dough on floured surface until smooth, enclose in plastic wrap; refrigerate 30 minutes.

PUMPKIN AND SWEET POTATO PIE

prep + cook time **1 hour 30 minutes (+ refrigeration & cooling)** serves **8**
nutritional count per serving **40.5g total fat (25.8g saturated fat); 2454kJ (587 cal); 49.2g carbohydrate; 7.7g protein; 2g fibre**

250g (8 ounces) coarsely chopped pumpkin
250g (8 ounces) coarsely chopped kumara (orange sweet potato)
½ cup (110g) firmly packed light brown sugar
1 teaspoon vanilla extract
1 teaspoon ground cinnamon
½ teaspoon each ground ginger and nutmeg
1 cup (250ml) pouring cream
2 eggs

pastry

1½ cups (225g) plain (all-purpose) flour
2 tablespoons icing (confectioners') sugar
125g (4 ounces) cold butter, chopped coarsely
1 egg yolk
2 tablespoons iced water, approximately

maple cream

1 cup (250ml) thickened (heavy) cream
2 tablespoons maple syrup

1 Make pastry. Grease 24cm (9½-inch) round loose-based flan tin.
2 Roll pastry between sheets of baking paper until large enough to line tin. Lift pastry into tin, press into side; trim edge. Refrigerate 20 minutes.
3 Preheat oven to 200°C/400°F. Place tin on oven tray; line pastry with baking paper, fill with dried beans or rice. Bake 10 minutes. Remove paper and beans; bake 10 minutes. Cool.
4 Reduce oven to 180°C/350°F.
5 Meanwhile, steam pumpkin and kumara, separately, until tender. Cool 10 minutes.
6 Blend or process pumpkin and kumara with remaining ingredients until smooth. Pour mixture into pastry case. Bake about 1 hour or until filling is set. Cool. Refrigerate until filling is firm.
7 Serve with maple cream.

pastry Process flour, icing sugar and butter until crumbly. Add egg yolk and enough of the water to make ingredients just come together. Knead dough on floured surface until smooth, enclose dough with plastic wrap; refrigerate 30 minutes.

maple cream Beat cream and syrup in small bowl with electric mixer until soft peaks form.

tips **It is important to steam, not boil, the pumpkin and kumara, to prevent vegetables becoming watery. Chop vegetables the same size so they cook evenly.**

CARAMEL PECAN PIE

prep + cook time **1 hour 20 minutes (+ refrigeration & cooling)** serves **8**
nutritional count per serving **31.1g total fat (13.2g saturated fat); 2094kJ (501 cal); 49g carbohydrate; 7.1g protein; 2.4g fibre**

½ cup (175g) golden syrup (or treacle)
¼ cup (55g) firmly packed light brown sugar
2 eggs, beaten lightly
50g (1½ ounces) butter, melted
2 tablespoons plain (all-purpose) flour
2 teaspoons vanilla extract
1 cup pecans (120g), toasted, halved

pastry

1½ cups (225g) plain (all-purpose) flour
2 tablespoons icing (confectioners') sugar
125g (4 ounces) cold butter, chopped coarsely
1 egg yolk
2 tablespoons iced water, approximately

1 Make pastry.
2 Roll pastry between sheets of baking paper until large enough to line 24cm (9½-inch) round loose-based flan tin. Ease pastry into tin, press into base and side; trim edge. Refrigerate 30 minutes.
3 Preheat oven to 200°C/400°F.
4 Place tin on oven tray. Line pastry with baking paper; fill with dried beans or rice. Bake 10 minutes; remove paper and beans. Bake 10 minutes; cool.
5 Reduce oven to 180°C/350°F.
6 Combine syrup, sugar, eggs, butter, flour and extract in small bowl; whisk until smooth. Pour mixture into pastry case; top with nuts.
7 Bake pie about 40 minutes or until set; cool.
pastry Process flour, icing sugar and butter until crumbly. Add egg yolk and enough of the water to make ingredients just come together. Knead dough on floured surface until smooth, enclose with plastic wrap; refrigerate 30 minutes.

COCONUT AND PASSIONFRUIT CUSTARD PIE

prep + cook time **1 hour 10 minutes** serves **8**
nutritional count per serving **23.8g total fat (15.6g saturated fat); 1647kJ (394 cal); 38.1g carbohydrate; 7g protein; 4.1g fibre**

- ½ cup (75g) plain (all-purpose) flour
- 1 cup (220g) caster (superfine) sugar
- 1 cup (80g) desiccated coconut
- 4 eggs, beaten lightly
- 2 teaspoons vanilla extract
- 125g (4 ounces) butter, melted
- 1⅓ cups (330ml) milk
- ½ cup (125ml) passionfruit pulp
- 1 tablespoon icing (confectioners') sugar

1 Preheat oven to 200°C/400°F. Grease straight-sided 24cm (9½-inch) pie dish.
2 Sift flour into large bowl; stir in sugar, coconut, egg, extract, butter, milk and passionfruit. Pour into dish.
3 Bake pie about 1 hour or until set.
4 Serve dusted with sifted icing sugar.

tips **You will need about six passionfruit for this recipe. A layer of custard will develop at the base of this pie during baking. Serve with whipped cream or ice-cream.**

LITTLE SALTY CARAMEL MERINGUE PIES

prep + cook time **1 hour (+ refrigeration & cooling)**
makes **8**
nutritional count per pie **17.9g total fat (11.4g saturated fat); 2195kJ (525 cal); 85.2g carbohydrate; 9.1g protein; 0.7g fibre**

395g (12½ ounces) canned sweetened condensed milk
30g (1 ounce) butter
¼ cup (90g) golden syrup (or treacle)
2 teaspoons sea salt flakes
¼ cup (60ml) pouring cream

pastry

1 cup (150g) plain (all-purpose) flour
⅓ cup (55g) icing (confectioners') sugar
90g (3 ounces) butter, chopped coarsely
1 egg yolk
1 tablespoon iced water, approximately

meringue

4 egg whites
1 cup (220g) caster (superfine) sugar

1 Make pastry.
2 Divide pastry into eight portions. Roll one portion at a time between sheets of baking paper until large enough to line eight 8cm (3-inch) loose-based flan tins. Ease pastry into tins, pressing into base and side; trim edges. Prick bases with fork. Place on oven tray; refrigerate 20 minutes.
3 Meanwhile, preheat oven to 180°C/350°F.
4 Line pastry with baking paper, fill with dried beans or rice. Bake 10 minutes; remove paper and beans. Bake about 5 minutes or until browned; cool.
5 Combine condensed milk, butter, syrup and salt in small heavy-based saucepan; stir over medium heat about 12 minutes or until caramel-coloured. Stir in cream. Spread filling into pastry cases.
6 Make meringue.
7 Spoon meringue onto tarts. Bake tarts about 5 minutes or until browned lightly.

pastry Process flour, icing sugar and butter until crumbly. Add egg yolk and most of the water; process until ingredients just come together. Knead pastry on floured surface until smooth, enclose with plastic wrap; refrigerate 30 minutes.

meringue Beat egg whites in small bowl with electric mixer until soft peaks form. Add sugar gradually, beating until dissolved between each addition.

VANILLA CUSTARD PIE

prep + cook time **40 minutes (+ refrigeration)** serves **10**
nutritional count per serving **29.4g total fat (13.8g saturated fat); 2178kJ (521 cal); 59g carbohydrate; 6.6g protein; 0.7g fibre**

2 sheets puff pastry
2 tablespoons icing (confectioners') sugar
¼ cup (20g) flaked almonds
1 cup (220g) caster (superfine) sugar
1 cup (150g) cornflour (cornstarch)
½ cup (60g) custard powder
1¼ cups (300ml) thickened (heavy) cream
3½ cups (875ml) milk
1 vanilla bean
60g (2 ounces) butter, chopped coarsely
2 egg yolks

1 Preheat oven to 220°C/425°F. Grease 24cm (9½-inch) round springform tin. Line oven trays with baking paper.
2 Place pastry sheets on oven trays; brush with a little water. Sprinkle evenly with sifted icing sugar. Sprinkle one pastry sheet with nuts. Bake about 15 minutes or until browned lightly. Gently flatten pastry with egg slice. Cut each sheet into 24cm (9½-inch) rounds. Place plain sheet in tin.
3 Meanwhile, combine caster sugar, cornflour and custard powder in medium saucepan. Combine cream and milk in large jug. Gradually stir milk mixture into sugar mixture, until smooth.
4 Halve vanilla bean lengthways, scrape seeds into pan; add butter. Bring to the boil over medium heat, stirring constantly until mixture boils and thickens. Simmer for 3 minutes, stirring constantly. Remove from heat; stir in egg yolks. Spread mixture over pastry in tin. Top with remaining pastry round, nut-side up. Refrigerate 2 hours or until firm.
5 Serve dusted with a little extra sifted icing sugar.

RHUBARB PIES WITH MERINGUE TOPPING

prep + cook time **55 minutes (+ cooling & refrigeration)**
makes **12**
nutritional count per pie **9.1g total fat (4.1g saturated fat); 794kJ (190 cal); 23.5g carbohydrate; 3.3g protein; 1.4g fibre**

1 bunch fresh rhubarb, trimmed (350g/11 ounces)
1 tablespoon caster (superfine) sugar
2 sheets shortcrust pastry
2 egg whites
½ cup (110g) caster (superfine) sugar, extra
1 tablespoon flaked almonds, chopped coarsely

1 Preheat oven to 200°C/400°F. Grease 12-hole (1½-tablespoon/30ml) shallow round-based patty pans.
2 Chop rhubarb into 2cm (¾-inch) cubes. Spread rhubarb onto baking-paper-lined oven tray; sprinkle with sugar. Bake, uncovered, about 10 minutes or until tender; cool.
3 Cut 12 x 7cm (2½-inch) rounds from pastry. Press rounds into pan holes; prick bases with fork. Refrigerate 20 minutes.
4 Bake pastry cases 10 minutes; cool.
5 Beat egg whites in small bowl with electric mixer until soft peaks form; gradually add extra sugar, beating until sugar dissolves.
6 Divide rhubarb filling between pastry cases. Spoon meringue over filling; sprinkle with nuts. Bake about 5 minutes or until browned lightly. Stand 5 minutes before serving.

tip **You can use one quantity shortcrust pastry (page 4) instead of the store-bought pastry sheets.**

ALLSPICE also called pimento or jamaican pepper; like a combination of nutmeg, cumin, clove and cinnamon. Available whole or ground.

BAKING PAPER also known as parchment paper or baking parchment – is a silicone-coated paper that is primarily used for lining baking pans and oven trays so cakes and biscuits won't stick, making removal easy.

BUTTER we use salted butter unless stated otherwise; 125g is equal to 1 stick (4 ounces).

CAPERS the grey-green buds of a warm climate (usually Mediterranean) shrub, sold either dried and salted or pickled in a vinegar brine; tiny young ones, called baby capers, are also available both in brine or dried in salt. Their pungent taste adds piquancy to tapenades, sauces and condiments.

CAPSICUM also called pepper or bell pepper. Discard seeds and membranes before use.

CHEESE

blue mould-treated cheeses mottled with blue veining. Varieties include firm and crumbly stilton types and mild, creamy brie-like cheeses.

cheddar is a relatively hard, yellow to off-white, and sometimes sharp cheese originally made in the English village of Cheddar, in Somerset.

fetta Greek in origin; a crumbly textured goat's- or sheep's-milk cheese having a sharp, salty taste. Ripened and stored in salted whey; particularly good cubed and tossed into salads.

manchego white to ivory cheese of Spanish origin usually made from sheep's milk.

parmesan also called parmigiano; a hard, grainy cow's milk cheese that originated in the Parma region of Italy. The curd for this cheese is salted in brine for a month, then aged for up to two years in humid conditions. Reggiano is the best parmesan, aged for a minimum of two years and made in the Italian region of Emilia-Romagna.

CHICKEN

breast fillet breast halved, skinned and boned.

tenderloin thin strip of meat from under the breast; good for stir-frying.

thigh fillet thigh with skin and centre bone removed.

CHIVES related to the onion and leek; have a subtle onion flavour. Used more for flavour than as an ingredient; chopped finely, used in sauces, dressings, omelettes or as a garnish.

CHORIZO sausage of Spanish origin, made of coarsely ground pork and seasoned with garlic and chilli. They are deeply smoked, very spicy and available fresh or dry-cured.

CINNAMON available both in the piece (called sticks or quills) and ground into powder; one of the world's most common spices, used universally as a sweet, fragrant flavouring for both sweet and savoury foods. The dried inner bark of the shoots of the Sri Lankan native cinnamon tree; much of what is sold as the real thing is in fact cassia, chinese cinnamon, from the cassia tree.

CORIANDER also called cilantro, pak chee or chinese parsley; bright-green-leafed herb with both pungent aroma and taste. Often stirred into or sprinkled over a dish just before serving for maximum impact as, like other leafy herbs, its characteristics diminish with cooking. Coriander seeds are dried and sold either whole or ground, and neither form tastes remotely like the fresh leaf.

CORNFLOUR also known as cornstarch. Available made from corn or wheat (wheaten cornflour gives a lighter texture in cakes); used as a thickening agent in cooking.

CREAM we use fresh cream, also known as pure or pouring cream unless otherwise stated. Contains no additives. Minimum fat content is 35 per cent.

sour a thick, commercially cultured sour cream with a minimum fat content of 35 per cent.

thick (double) a dolloping cream with fat content of around 45 per cent.

thickened (heavy) a whipping cream containing thickener. Minimum fat content 35 per cent.

CUMIN also known as zeera or comino; resembling caraway in size, cumin is the dried seed of a plant related to the parsley family. Its spicy, almost curry-like flavour is essential to the traditional foods of Mexico, India, North Africa and the Middle East. Available dried as seeds or ground. Black cumin seeds are smaller than standard cumin, and dark brown rather than true black; they are mistakenly confused with kalonji (black onion seeds).

GLOSSARY

CURRY PASTES

butter chicken a mildly spiced rich paste from the North Indian state of Punjab. The combination of tomato and fenugreek leaves gives the paste its distinctive flavour.

green the hottest of the traditional pastes; particularly good in chicken and vegetable curries, and a great addition to stir-fries and noodle dishes.

EGGPLANT also called aubergine. Ranging in size from tiny to very large and in colour from pale green to deep purple. Can also be purchased char-grilled, packed in oil, in jars.

EGGS we use large chicken eggs weighing an average of 60g unless stated otherwise in the recipes in this book. If a recipe calls for raw or barely cooked eggs, exercise caution if there is a salmonella problem in your area, particularly in food eaten by children and pregnant women.

FENNEL also called finocchio or anise; a crunchy green vegetable slightly resembling celery that's eaten raw in salads, fried as an accompaniment, or used as an ingredient in soups and sauces. Also the name given to the dried seeds of the plant which have a stronger licorice flavour.

FIVE-SPICE POWDER although the ingredients vary from country to country, five-spice is usually a fragrant mixture of ground cinnamon, cloves, star anise, sichuan pepper and fennel seeds. Used in Chinese and other Asian cooking; available from most supermarkets or Asian food shops.

FRENCH-STYLE GREEN LENTILS related to the famous French puy lentils; these green-blue, tiny lentils have a nutty, earthy flavour and a hardy nature that allows them to be rapidly cooked without disintegrating. Are also known as australian, bondi or matilda lentils.

GNOCCHI Italian 'dumplings' made of potatoes, semolina or flour; can be boiled or baked with sauce.

GREEN ONION also known as scallion or (incorrectly) shallot; an immature onion picked before the bulb has formed, with a long, bright-green edible stalk.

HARISSA a North African paste made from dried red chillies, garlic, olive oil and caraway seeds; can be used as a rub for meat, an ingredient in sauces and dressings, or eaten as a condiment for tagines and grills.

KAFFIR LIME LEAVES also known as *bai magrood* and looks like two glossy dark green leaves joined end to end, forming a rounded hourglass shape. Sold fresh, dried or frozen, the dried leaves are less potent so double the number if using them as a substitute for fresh; a strip of fresh lime peel may be substituted for each kaffir lime leaf.

KUMARA the Polynesian name of an orange-fleshed sweet potato often confused with yam; good baked, boiled, mashed or fried similarly to other potatoes.

LEEKS a member of the onion family, the leek resembles a green onion but is much larger and more subtle in flavour. Tender baby or pencil leeks can be eaten whole with minimal cooking but adult leeks are usually trimmed of most of the green tops then chopped or sliced and cooked as an ingredient in stews and soups.

MAPLE SYRUP distilled from the sap of sugar maple trees found only in Canada and about 10 states in the USA. Maple-flavoured syrup or pancake syrup is not an adequate substitute for the real thing.

MILK we always use full-cream homogenised milk unless specified.

buttermilk in spite of its name, buttermilk is actually low in fat, varying between 0.6 per cent and 2.0 per cent per 100ml. Originally the term given to the slightly sour liquid left after butter was churned from cream, today it is intentionally made from no-fat or low-fat milk. Because it is low in fat, it's a good substitute for dairy products such as cream or sour cream in some baking and salad dressings.

PAPRIKA ground dried sweet red capsicum (bell pepper); many grades and types are available, including sweet, hot, mild and smoked.

PASTRY, PACKAGED

fillo is unique in that no fat or margarine is added to the dough. The dough is very elastic in texture and not rolled like other pastries but stretched to the desired thickness. Brush with butter or oil before baking.

puff pastry packaged sheets of frozen puff pastry, available from supermarkets.

shortcrust pastry packaged sheets of frozen shortcrust pastry, available from supermarkets.

PISTACHIOS green, delicately flavoured nuts inside hard off-white shells. Available salted or unsalted.

POLENTA also called cornmeal; a flour-like cereal made of dried corn (maize). Also the dish made from it.

QUINCE yellow-skinned fruit with hard texture and astringent, tart taste; eaten cooked or as a preserve. Long, slow cooking makes the flesh a deep rose pink.

ROCKET also called arugula, rugula and rucola; peppery green leaf eaten raw in salads or used in cooking. Baby rocket leaves are smaller and less peppery in flavour.

ROSE PETALS freeze-dried rose petals are edible and make great cake and dessert decorations.

SAFFRON stigma of a member of the crocus family, available ground or in strands; imparts a yellow-orange colour to food once infused. The quality can vary greatly; the best is the most expensive spice in the world.

SAUCES

plum a thick, sweet and sour dipping sauce made from plums, vinegar, sugar, chillies and spices.

soy also known as sieu; made from fermented soybeans. Several varieties are available in supermarkets and Asian food stores; we use japanese soy sauce unless indicated otherwise.

worcestershire thin, dark-brown spicy sauce developed by the British when in India; used as a seasoning for meat, gravies and cocktails, and also as a condiment.

SEAFOOD

blue-eye also known as deep sea trevalla or trevally and blue-eye cod; thick, moist white-fleshed fish.

ling a member of the cod family with white, firm, moist flesh; fillets are nearly boneless.

prawns also known as shrimp. Varieties include, school, king, royal red, sydney harbour, tiger. Can be bought uncooked (green) or cooked, with or without shells.

smoked cod white fish with a milky smoky flavour; skin is orange coloured.

white fish means non-oily fish; includes bream, flathead, whiting, snapper, dhufish, redfish and ling.

SESAME SEEDS black and white are the most common of this small oval seed, however there are also red and brown varieties. The seeds are used as an ingredient and as a condiment. Roast the seeds in a heavy-based frying pan over low heat.

SHALLOTS also called french shallots, golden shallots or eschalots. Small and elongated, with a brown-skin, they grow in tight clusters similar to garlic.

SILVER BEET also known as swiss chard and incorrectly, spinach; has fleshy stalks and large leaves, both of which can be prepared as for spinach.

SPECK smoked pork.

SPINACH also known as english spinach and incorrectly, silver beet. Baby spinach leaves are best eaten raw in salads; the larger leaves should be added last to soups, stews and stir-fries, and should be cooked until barely wilted.

SUGAR we use coarse, granulated table sugar, also known as crystal sugar, unless otherwise specified.

brown, light a soft, finely granulated sugar retaining molasses for its characteristic colour and flavour.

caster also known as superfine or finely granulated table sugar.

demerara small-grained golden-coloured crystal sugar.

icing also known as confectioners' sugar or powdered sugar; pulverised granulated sugar crushed together with a small amount of cornflour.

TAHINI sesame seed paste available from Middle Eastern food stores.

TOMATOES

bottled tomato pasta sauce a prepared tomato-based sauce (sometimes called ragu or sugo on the label); comes in varying degrees of thickness and kinds of spicing.

canned whole peeled tomatoes in natural juices.

egg also called plum or roma, these are smallish, oval-shaped tomatoes much used in Italian cooking or salads.

paste triple-concentrated tomato puree used to flavour soups, stews, sauces and casseroles.

sauce also known as ketchup.

WHITE BEANS a generic term we use for canned or dried cannellini, haricot, navy or great northern beans belonging to the same family, *Phaseolus vulgaris*.

YEAST (dried and fresh), a raising agent used in dough making.

YOGURT we use plain full-cream in our recipes unless specificially noted otherwise. If a recipe in this book calls for low-fat yogurt, we use one with a fat content of less than 0.2 per cent.

ZUCCHINI also called courgette; small, pale- or dark-green or yellow vegetable of the squash family. Harvested when young, its edible flowers can be stuffed with a mild cheese and deep-fried.

CONVERSION CHART

MEASURES

One Australian metric measuring cup holds approximately 250ml, one Australian metric tablespoon holds 20ml, one Australian metric teaspoon holds 5ml.

The difference between one country's measuring cups and another's is within a 2- or 3-teaspoon variance, and will not affect your cooking results. North America, New Zealand and the United Kingdom use a 15ml tablespoon. All cup and spoon measurements are level. The most accurate way of measuring dry ingredients is to weigh them. When measuring liquids, use a clear glass or plastic jug with metric markings.

We use large eggs with an average weight of 60g.

DRY MEASURES

METRIC	IMPERIAL
15g	½oz
30g	1oz
60g	2oz
90g	3oz
125g	4oz (¼lb)
155g	5oz
185g	6oz
220g	7oz
250g	8oz (½lb)
280g	9oz
315g	10oz
345g	11oz
375g	12oz (¾lb)
410g	13oz
440g	14oz
470g	15oz
500g	16oz (1lb)
750g	24oz (1½lb)
1kg	32oz (2lb)

LIQUID MEASURES

METRIC	IMPERIAL
30ml	1 fluid oz
60ml	2 fluid oz
100ml	3 fluid oz
125ml	4 fluid oz
150ml	5 fluid oz
190ml	6 fluid oz
250ml	8 fluid oz
300ml	10 fluid oz
500ml	16 fluid oz
600ml	20 fluid oz
1000ml (1 litre)	1¾ pints

LENGTH MEASURES

METRIC	IMPERIAL
3mm	⅛in
6mm	¼in
1cm	½in
2cm	¾in
2.5cm	1in
5cm	2in
6cm	2½in
8cm	3in
10cm	4in
13cm	5in
15cm	6in
18cm	7in
20cm	8in
23cm	9in
25cm	10in
28cm	11in
30cm	12in (1ft)

OVEN TEMPERATURES

These oven temperatures are only a guide for conventional ovens. For fan-forced ovens, check the manufacturer's manual.

	°C (CELSIUS)	°F (FAHRENHEIT)
Very slow	120	250
Slow	150	275-300
Moderately slow	160	325
Moderate	180	350-375
Moderately hot	200	400
Hot	220	425-450
Very hot	240	475

The imperial measurements used in these recipes are approximate only. Measurements for cake pans are approximate only.

INDEX

Published in 2012 by ACP Books, Sydney

ACP Books are published by ACP Magazines Limited,
a division of Nine Entertainment Co.

54 Park St, Sydney
GPO Box 4088, Sydney, NSW 2001.

phone (+61)(2) 9282 8618; fax (+61)(2) 9126 3702

acpbooks@acpmagazines.com.au; www.acpbooks.com.au

ACP BOOKS

General Manager - Christine Whiston

Editor-in-Chief - Susan Tomnay

Creative Director - Hieu Chi Nguyen

Food Director - Pamela Clark

Published and Distributed in the United Kingdom by Octopus Publishing Group

Endeavour House

189 Shaftesbury Avenue

London WC2H 8JY

United Kingdom

phone (+44)(0)207 632 5400; fax (+44)(0)207 632 5405

info@octopus-publishing.co.uk;

www.octopusbooks.co.uk

Printed by Toppan Printing Co., China

International Foreign Language Rights, Brian Cearnes, ACP Books bcearnes@acpmagazines.com.au

A catalogue record for this book is available from the British Library.

ISBN 978-1-74245-238-8